Gus's Black Feathers

By Sally Cowan

Josh and Beth got
Gus the gull to the vet.

His wing was in a blob
of black net.

"Can you fix it?" said Beth.

"I will cut away this big blob of net," said Ming, the vet.

"This net is a big mess," Ming said.

I have to cut some black feathers.

Ming cut some black
feathers off Gus's wing.

Gus bled a little,
and he yelled!

"I will blot it," said Ming.

"He can not flap his wing yet," said Ming.

In two days, Gus was well.

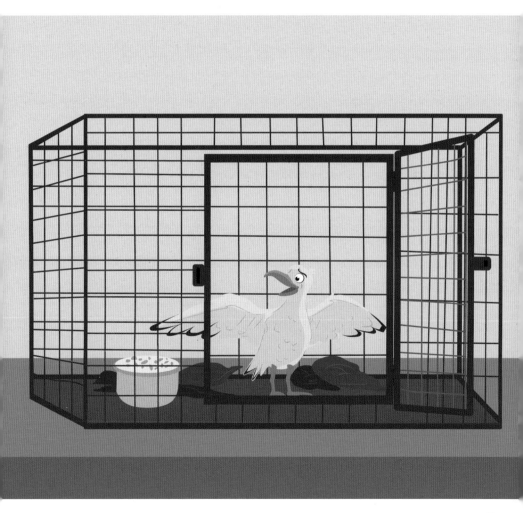

"He can go home," said Ming.
"You did a good thing!"

"Do not blush, Beth!"
said Josh.

At the rocks, Gus went
up and up.

His wings went *flap, flap*
till he was a black dot.

CHECKING FOR MEANING

1. Why did Gus need to go to the vet? *(Literal)*

2. Why did Ming need to cut away some of Gus's feathers? *(Literal)*

3. Why was Gus a black dot at the end of the story? *(Inferential)*

EXTENDING VOCABULARY

bled	What does *bled* mean? What did Gus's feathers do if we say they bled? What are other words that belong to this word family? E.g. bleed, bleeding, blood.
blot	When might you need to *blot* something? How do you blot something? What do you need to do this?
flap	Look at the word *flap*. How many letters are in this word? How many sounds are there?

MOVING BEYOND THE TEXT

1. Why do birds and other animals get caught in nets?

2. Where are these nets? Why are they there?

3. How did Josh and Beth act responsibly when they found Gus?

4. What makes people blush? Talk about a time when you blushed and why.

SPEED SOUNDS

bl	gl	cr	fr	st

PRACTICE WORDS

black

blob

bled

block

blot

blush